GETTING TO KNOW
THE U.S. PRESIDENTS

RUTHERFORD B.
HAYES

NINETEENTH PRESIDENT
1877 – 1881

WRITTEN AND ILLUSTRATED BY MIKE VENEZIA

CHILDREN'S PRESS®
A DIVISION OF SCHOLASTIC INC.
NEW YORK   TORONTO   LONDON   AUCKLAND   SYDNEY
MEXICO CITY   NEW DELHI   HONG KONG
DANBURY, CONNECTICUT

Reading Consultant: Nanci R. Vargus, Ed.D., Assistant Professor, School of Education, University of Indianapolis

Historical Consultant: Marc J. Selverstone, Ph.D., Assistant Professor, Miller Center of Public Affairs, University of Virginia

Photographs © 2006: Corbis Images: 8 (Beach & Bodurtha), 13, 30 (Bettmann), 17; Library of Congress: 22 (Brady Civil War Photograph Collection), 3 (Brady-Handy Collection); North Wind Picture Archives: 15; PictureHistory.com: 27; Rutherford B. Hayes Presidential Center, Fremont, Ohio: 6, 10, 12, 14, 18, 29, 32; Stock Montage, Inc.: 24; Superstock, Inc.: 16; The Art Archive/Picture Desk/Culver Pictures: 23.

Colorist for illustrations: Dave Ludwig

Library of Congress Cataloging-in-Publication Data

Venezia, Mike.
   Rutherford B. Hayes / written and illustrated by Mike Venezia.
      p. cm. — (Getting to know the U.S. presidents)
   ISBN 0-516-22624-X (lib. bdg.)   0-516-25404-9   (pbk.)
   1. Hayes, Rutherford Birchard, 1822-1893—Juvenile literature. 2.
Presidents—United States—Biography—Juvenile literature. I. Title.
   E682.V46 2006
   973.8'3'092—dc22

                              2005012082

CHILDREN'S PRESS and associated logos are trademarks
and/or registered trademarks of Scholastic Library Publishing.
SCHOLASTIC and associated logos are trademarks and/or
registered trademarks of Scholastic Inc.

1 2 3 4 5 6 7 8 9 10 R 15 14 13 12 11 10 09 08 07 06

A photograph of Rutherford B. Hayes

Rutherford B. Hayes, the nineteenth president of the United States, was born on October 4, 1822, in Delaware, Ohio. Ulysses S. Grant was president right before Hayes. President Grant had hired some friends who turned out to be shady and crooked. An honest, upstanding man like Rutherford was just what the country needed to get things back in shape again.

In 1876, Republican candidate Rutherford B. Hayes ran against Democratic candidate Samuel Tilden. Both men were honest, but a few of the people who worked to get them into office were not. Some political leaders at the time used their government jobs to gain power or steal money from the public.

During one of the closest presidential races in history, both sides did nasty things to try to make sure their man would win. This was exactly the type of activity Rutherford B. Hayes was determined to stop when he became president.

A portrait of Sophia Hayes,
the mother of Rutherford B. Hayes

While growing up, Rutherford B. Hayes was called Rud by his family and friends. Rud was so weak and sick when he was born that nobody thought he'd live very long. Mrs. Hayes was very worried. She had already lost a daughter, and Rud's father had died of a fever just ten weeks before Rud was born. Then, when Rud was only two, his older brother drowned in an ice-skating accident.

Mrs. Hayes decided to shelter her only remaining son from harm. She showered him with attention. Rud wasn't allowed to go outside and play sports until he was nine years old. Rud's main playmate and best friend was his older sister, Fanny. Fanny also agreed that her only brother should be treated very carefully.

Rutherford B. Hayes was born in this house in Delaware, Ohio.

The Hayes family was able to get along pretty well money-wise. Mrs. Hayes earned income from a farm the family owned outside Delaware, Ohio. Rud and Fanny had a generous uncle, too. Uncle Sardis Birchard helped pay for his niece's and nephew's schooling. Uncle Sardis always encouraged Rud. Fanny, too, always urged Rud to become someone important.

When Fanny and Rud started school, they quickly learned to study hard and to obey their teacher, Mr. Granger. Mr. Granger was a thin, ferocious man who whipped misbehaving students, even if they were twice his size. He said that if any student fooled around, he'd throw them through the wall of the schoolhouse. Once he threw a large jackknife, just missing a boy who was whispering to Rud!

Rutherford B. Hayes as a young man

Rud became an excellent student. While in college, he decided to be a lawyer. After graduating from Harvard Law School, he opened his own law office in Lower Sandusky, Ohio, the small town where Uncle Sardis lived. Rud soon realized he could be more successful in a big city, so he moved to Cincinnati, Ohio.

Rud opened a new law office there with another young lawyer. Neither man had a place to live, so both slept in the office until they could afford apartments.

People in Cincinnati started to hear about Rud Hayes. He was never afraid to defend runaway slaves who had escaped from the South. He was proud to defend any poor, needy person whose rights had been ignored.

The wedding portrait of Rutherford and Lucy Webb Hayes

During this time, Rud began visiting a girl he had met in his hometown years before. Lucy Webb was from a well-respected family. She was one of few women at the time who had gone to college. Rud's mother and his sister Fanny really liked Lucy. They were thrilled when Rud asked Lucy to marry him.

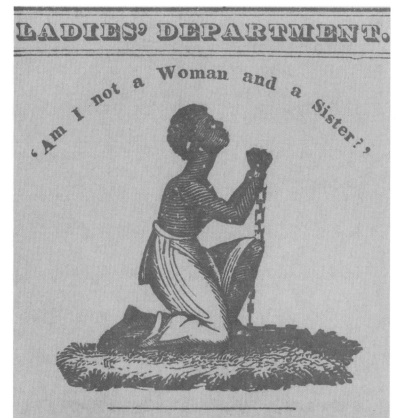

'Am I not a Woman and a Sister?'

White Lady, happy, proud and free,
Lend awhile thine ear to me ;
Let the Negro Mother's wail
Turn thy pale cheek still more pale.
Can the Negro Mother joy
Over this her captive boy,
Which in bondage and in tears,
For a life of wo she rears ?
Though she bears a Mother's name,
A Mother's rights she may not claim ;
For the white man's will can part,
Her darling from her bursting heart.

From the Genius of Universal Emancipation
LETTERS ON SLAVERY.—No. III.

Lucy Hayes believed strongly in abolition. She sided with those who wrote anti-slavery poems like this one.

Rud and Lucy got married in 1852. Right away they began to raise a large family. Lucy believed strongly in women's rights and in abolition. Northern abolitionists wanted to stop slavery immediately in the southern states. They also worked to prevent slavery from spreading into new U.S. territories. Lucy influenced her husband to care about these causes.

In 1856,
Fanny, the
sister Rud
loved so much,
died unexpectedly.
Rud was so sad he could
hardly do a thing for weeks. Rud finally
took his mind off the tragedy by getting
involved in politics. When the head lawyer
for the city of Cincinnati died in 1858,
Rud managed to fill in for him until the
next election.

This illustration shows how Cincinnati looked when Rutherford B. Hayes practiced law there in the mid-1800s.

Rud did so well at the job that he easily won the election for the next term as city attorney. Rutherford B. Hayes set high standards. He treated people fairly and honestly and was well respected as the city's top legal expert.

Abraham Lincoln was determined to keep the United States together as one nation.

Rud was enjoying life more than ever. He now had three sons and Lucy was expecting a fourth. But life would soon change for Rud. In 1861, Abraham Lincoln became president. It was a terrible time in United States history. For years there had been a huge disagreement between northern and southern states.

People in the North wanted to end or limit slavery in the United States. People in the South wanted to have the right to own black slaves. Soon after Abe Lincoln was elected, southern states decided to break away from the Union and form their own country—the Confederate States of America. This was totally unacceptable to people in the North. The decision soon led to the worst war in America's history.

The Civil War began when Confederate troops attacked Fort Sumter on April 12, 1861.

Major Rutherford B. Hayes (far left) with the 23rd Ohio Volunteer Infantry

President Lincoln immediately called for volunteers to help fight in the Civil War. Rutherford B. Hayes was so outraged about the South splitting the country apart that he joined the 23rd Ohio Volunteer Infantry. Even though he was nearly forty years old, he insisted on fighting right along with everyone else. After Rud's training period, the governor of Ohio made him a major.

Major Hayes and his men were sent to mountain areas in the western part of Virginia. His men patrolled roads and chased the enemy out of hiding places.

Rud quickly learned about warfare. He found that he loved the rugged outdoors, marching through hills, and camping out at night. He was probably enjoying all the outdoor activities he had missed out on while growing up.

People who knew Rutherford B. Hayes were surprised by the change that came over him when he was in combat. Ordinarily, Rud was known as a thoughtful, quiet, and loving family man. During battles, he suddenly became a ferocious fighter. Rud's men trusted and respected their daring leader.

Major Hayes always fought alongside his men. He was wounded time after time. Soon, he was promoted to major general. General Hayes' friends in Ohio thought the popular Rud should run for Congress. Rud eventually agreed to run, and was elected to the U.S. House of Representatives while he was still fighting in the war.

During the Reconstruction period, the U.S. government tried to help the South recover from the damage done by the Civil War (above). Rutherford B. Hayes served in Congress during this time.

In 1865, after four years of bloody civil war, the North finally won. Abe Lincoln was anxious to get the country back together again. His plan to do this was called Reconstruction.

Abe never got the chance to carry out his plan. Only five days after the Civil War ended, Abraham Lincoln was assassinated.

Rud began his new job in Congress at this time. After serving as a U.S. Representative for two years, he was elected governor of Ohio. He was an honest, skillful leader who always did a good job. Members of the Republican party thought Rud might make a good presidential candidate. In 1876, Rutherford B. Hayes agreed to run for U.S. president.

A campaign poster from the 1876 presidential election

After a very close election, Rutherford B. Hayes became the nineteenth president of the United States. One of the first things he did as president was remove federal troops from southern states.

Federal troops had been sent to the South right after the Civil War. They were there to make sure state governments were set up properly and that former slaves were treated fairly. These troops remained in the South for twelve years.

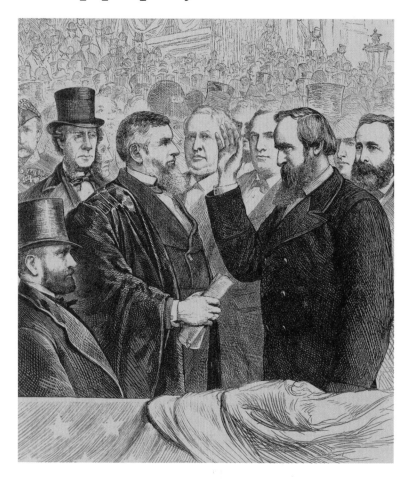

An illustration showing Rutherford B. Hayes being sworn in as president

People from the southern states always hated having Union army soldiers looking over their shoulders. During his presidential campaign, Hayes had promised that if he became president, he would remove federal troops from the South. In return, the southern leaders promised that they would uphold the rights of African Americans.

President Hayes thought government leaders in the South would be thankful the soldiers were leaving. He hoped this decision would help mend hard feelings and bring the country back together again.

Unfortunately, white southern leaders soon went back to their old tricks. They took power back from elected black leaders by voting them out of their government jobs. They did everything they could to prevent blacks from voting and refused to protect their rights. They kept African Americans from using the same schools, restaurants, stores, and bathrooms as white people. Separating white and black citizens this way is known as segregation.

After Reconstruction, the lives of southern black sharecroppers weren't much better than they had been before the Civil War.

Although white southern leaders were happier, black citizens weren't much better off than they had been before the Civil War. President Hayes was disappointed. He didn't like what was happening, but there wasn't much he could do about it.

Still, Rutherford B. Hayes turned out to be a good leader. He worked hard to pass laws that would keep lazy, crooked people out of government jobs. He helped the United States get out of a serious money problem called a depression.

President Hayes, Lucy, and their children turned the White House into a happy, lively place. Lucy hosted wonderful parties there, and she and President Hayes started the tradition of the White House Easter Egg Roll. Because the First Lady never allowed alcoholic drinks in the White House, she became known as "Lemonade Lucy."

President and Mrs. Hayes started the tradition of the annual
White House Easter Egg Roll.

In the 1870s, when Rutherford B. Hayes was president, thousands of Immigrants came to the United States to seek better lives.

President Hayes took office during a time of great change in the United States. Women were beginning to demand the right to vote. Hundreds of thousands of people arrived from countries around the world. They hoped to find jobs and a better life in the United States.

It seemed as if amazing machines and devices of all kinds were being invented every day. President Hayes was the first president to have a telephone installed in the White House. The only problem was that hardly anyone else had a telephone yet so there was no one around for him to call.

Rutherford B. Hayes
(with gray beard)
surrounded by
members of his
family

Rutherford B. Hayes had promised he would serve only one four-year term as president. In 1881, he and his family left Washington, D.C., and returned to their home in Ohio.

When Rutherford took office, two past presidents and a bunch of greedy politicians had left the presidency in its weakest condition ever. Only an outstanding, honest man like Hayes could have brought respect back to the office of president. Rutherford B. Hayes lived out a peaceful life at his large home in Ohio. He died there on January 17, 1893.